Fighter Pilot

The Photographic Kaleidoscope

Lady Bader

Lindmann
616 Sqn

Best Wishes
Robert J. Rudhell

J V Roberts
19 and 151 Sqns

R H Paues
bee 19 Sqn

19 & 81 Sqn

E J Carter
81 Squadron (Pilot)

Peter J. Foot
56 & 234 Sq.

Keith Lawrence
234 603 Sqns & 421 Flt

Bob Morris 66 Sqns

A Williamson
616 & 19

Fighter Pilot

The Photographic Kaleidoscope

Dilip Sarkar

Ramrod Publications

Other books by Dilip Sarkar:-

SPITFIRE SQUADRON: *19 Squadron at War 1939-41*
THE INVISIBLE THREAD: *A Spitfire's Tale*
THROUGH PERIL TO THE STARS
ANGRIFF WESTLAND
A FEW OF THE MANY: *A Kaleidoscope of Memories*
BADER'S TANGMERE SPITFIRES: *The Untold Story, 1941*

BADER'S DUXFORD FIGHTERS: *The Big Wing Controversy*
MISSING IN ACTION: *Resting in Peace?*
GUARDS VC: *Blitzkrieg 1940*
BATTLE OF BRITAIN: *The Photographic Kaleidoscope Volume I*
BATTLE OF BRITAIN: *The Photographic Kaleidoscope Volume II*
BATTLE OF BRITAIN: *The Photographic Kaleidoscope Volume III*

To receive details of other books published by Ramrod Publications, please send to the address shown below.

Dilip's *Douglas Bader: The Legend Lives On* follows in August 2001 (published by The Douglas Bader Foundation), and his long-awaited *Johnnie's Kenley Spitfires* will hopefully be released in 2002.

FIGHTER PILOT: *The Photographic Kaleidoscope* © **Dilip Sarkar, 2001.**

First published 2001 by Ramrod Publications, 16 Kingfisher Close, St Peter's, Worcester WR5 3RY, ENGLAND. Tel & Fax: 01905 767735, email: anita@ramrodbooks.u-net.com.

ISBN: 0-9538539-2-6
Layout & Design by Ramrod Publications.
Printed in Great Britain by The Cromwell Press, Trowbridge, Wiltshire.

Dedication

This book is respectfully dedicated to the memory of a special friend, the late Flight Lieutenant Ron Rayner DFC RAF (Ret'd), from whom I learned so much about the way of a fighter pilot.

Acknowledgements

Firstly, we are most grateful to that wartime favourite Dame Vera Lynn for so kindly writing the Foreword to this book; a marvellous lady, still a favourite over half a century later!

Grateful thanks are also extended to all of those friends, including veterans, relatives of casualties and fellow enthusiasts, who have so kindly supported my research over the years. Without this invaluable assistance, such books would not be possible.

Again as ever, Andrew Long deserves a special mention for his photographic work, as does occasional but excellent aviation poet Larry McHale, whose enthusiasm is always a tonic.

My wife's commitment to make Ramrod Publications the success that it is today has finally brought my vision to reality, so to Anita goes the greatest thanks of all. The conditions under which this particular book was produced, given that our home was virtually destroyed by water damage, make Anita's efforts both even more appreciated and astonishing!

Contents

Foreword

'Coming in on a Wing and a Prayer' was a popular song during the war years, and one that I sang myself. It conveyed what we all felt when we saw our boys safely return to base. We owe them so much, and books like this, written and produced by young people born long after 1945, do much to keep the memory alive. Hopefully this book will therefore achieve the success that it deserves.

Dame Vera Lynn, D.B.E., LL.D., M.Mus
Sussex, February 2001

The Forces' Favourite: ENSA star Vera Lynn pictured in Calcutta, 1944. Still a favourite now, nearly 60 years on!

Photograph courtesy of Dame Vera Lynn

Author's Introduction

When considering the immensely high-tech military aircraft of today, it is a remarkable fact that man's first powered flight was made less than 100 years ago. In 1903, the Wright brothers made that historic flight in America. Just six years later Louis Bleriot, a Frenchman, flew across the English Channel. The opportunities for travel and communication offered by flight was immeasurable, but it was only a question of time before man harnessed this new frontier to military objectives.

At first many in the military were suspicious of aeroplanes. During the First World War, however, the aircraft's potential as an airborne observation post was soon realised by both sides. It was the start of an apparently never-ending arms race. The Allies attempted to destroy German reconnaissance aircraft and vice-versa. Aircrew were first armed with rifles and pistols, then machine-guns designed for ground warfare were adapted for use in the air. Designers began creating military aeroplanes with specific roles in mind: fighters, reconnaissance and bomber aircraft. It was not until the mid-1930s, however, when the Nazi *Luftwaffe obliterated* the Spanish City of Guernica, that the true potential of air power was realised. This generated a fear of bombers akin to the post war dread of nuclear weapons. Not surprisingly, therefore, the emphasis was placed not on fighters but on bombers, which were considered to be a new super weapon.

Nevertheless, the Great War had made a star of the fighter pilot. Despite the comparatively limited performance of their craft, in contemporary terms these men flew the Harriers of their day. In propaganda the fighter pilot cut a dashing figure, and the media created the 'ace', a status achieved by the destruction of five or more enemy aircraft. Both sides well publicised the exploits of their leading 'aces', but it is fair to say that one man eclipsed all others: Manfred *Freiherr* von Richthofen, better known as the 'Red Baron'. Von Richthofen himself was killed in aerial combat near Sailly-le-Sac, France, on April 21st, 1918; despite his 84 victories, the 'Red Baron' was only 22-years old at the time of his own violent death. All combatant nations had their fighter pilot heroes during the Great War, however, and these men would inspire a whole new generation of young men also willing to fly and fight in the service of King and country.

Between the wars the intention of most governments was to disarm, and so there was little spending on either the development or manufacture of military aircraft. Even as late as 1938, for example, many RAF squadrons remained equipped with biplane aircraft similar in both appearance and performance to those flown between 1914-18. The emphasis of what little spending there was had been on the bomber force. Lord Trenchard, the 'Father of the Royal Air Force', himself believed aircraft to be 'the most offensive weapon that has ever been invented. It is a shockingly bad weapon for defence'. He went on to say that he considered fighters valuable only for the purpose of 'keeping up the morale of your own people'.

Fortunately, others disagreed, not least due to developments in Germany, including the advent of the Me 109 that heralded a new generation of modern fighter aircraft. The '109' was a single-engined monoplane fighter that was both manoeuvrable and well armed. The British response was two similar fighters, the names of which are now legendary: Spitfire and Hurricane.

Although brought up in the shadow of a further war with Germany, in 1939 there was no shortage of young men eager to climb into the cockpit of an RAF fighter. All were volunteers, but their routes varied. Some were pre-war airmen, largely commissioned officers but with a smaller number of professional NCOs. Others had learned to fly at weekends with the RAF Volunteer Reserve, others with the Auxiliary Air Force before being called up for full-time service. The universities also provided pilots through the University Air Squadrons. However, if not for the outbreak of war in September 1939, very few of these young men would have actually become fighter pilots. In many ways they were ordinary young men plunged into exceptional circumstances. They responded accordingly, their deeds now also legendary.

Richard Hillary is a case in point. Whilst at Trinity College, Oxford, he learned to fly with the University Air Squadron, his desire being to become a fighter pilot. In his classic first-hand account *The Last Enemy*, Hillary, an intellectual, describes the appeal:-

For in a Spitfire we're back to war as it ought to be… Back to individual combat, to self-reliance, total responsibility for one's own fate. One either kills or is killed; and it's damned exciting.

He also describes the prelude to his first Spitfire flight:-

The Spitfires stood in two lines outside 'A' Flight pilots' room. The dull grey-brown of the camouflage could not conceal the clear-cut beauty, the wicked simplicity of their lines. I hooked up my parachute and climbed awkwardly into the low cockpit. I noticed how small was my field of vision. Kilmartin swung himself on to a wing and started to run through the instruments. I was conscious of his voice, but heard nothing of what he said. I was to fly a Spitfire. It was what I had most wanted through all the long dreary months of training. If I could fly a Spitfire, it would be worth it.

The appeal of fighters was not limited to pilots alone. In May 1940, 18-year old Bob Morris found himself posted from the RAF Technical School at Halton to No 66 (F) Squadron at Coltishall in Norfolk:-

My first glimpse of 66 Squadron was from the bus that travelled alongside the airfield. What a thrill to see Spitfires, this was every young man's dream!

Already, Hawker Hurricane equipped fighter squadrons were in action over France in a vain attempt to stop the Nazi *Blitzkrieg*. After the Fall of France came the Battle of Britain, when many young RAF pilots, including Richard Hillary, would give their lives in the defence of their homeland. Casualties also saw the composition of fighter squadrons change. Foreign nationals from the occupied lands, such as free Poles, French, Belgians and Czechs, joined the ranks of RAF Fighter Command, and regular units began to admit replacements from the VR. Locally raised Auxiliary squadrons not surprisingly found casualties hard to deal with, replacements from the regular service and VR diluting their strong, family-like, atmosphere.

Gone forever was the RAF's pre-war 'strawberries and cream' period during which, it has often been said, the service represented an elitist flying club.

The Battle of Britain saw the first time that a decision could have been forced through an aerial campaign. The Germans failed, however, in their determined attempt to wrest aerial supremacy over England from the RAF as a prelude to a seaborne invasion. In achieving this victory, the 'Few' ensured that Britain remained a base from which war against Germany could be waged, this being the key to ultimate victory. The night blitz, however, raged throughout the autumn and winter of 1940, lasting until the spring of 1941. In Britain's night skies was fought out a deadly game of cat and mouse, as RAF aircrews stalked the raiders. As the RAF struggled with their embryonic Airborne Interception systems, it was a frustrating and bitter battle.

In 1941, Britain naturally anticipated a resumption of Germany's efforts to invade, but in June Hitler invaded Soviet Russia. This changed the emphasis from the west to the east, but in any event Fighter Command was poised to go on the offensive. By this time improved Spitfires were replacing Hurricanes and were reaching most front line RAF squadrons. The Spitfire, however, was not designed as an offensive fighter, so in a reversal of 1940 it was now Fighter Command that faced two sea-crossings, often escorting small formations of bombers, whilst the Me 109 was used in its intended role. Pure fighter sweeps had already been discovered to be of limited value, so the bombers were essential in provoking a reaction from the defenders. With numerous RAF squadrons airborne, the plan was that the enemy fighters would be destroyed en masse. The reality would be quite different.

Given that there were no targets in France crucial to the Nazi war effort, the Germans were able to pick and choose when and where they engaged. This put the RAF at an enormous disadvantage and losses were high. Amongst those casualties were experienced pilots and leaders, the loss of whom were bitter blows. Air Commodore Sir Archie Winskill remembers:-

In 1941, I was flying Spitfires with 41 Squadron as a part of the Tangmere Wing. On August 14th, however, I was shot down on what was the first sweep after we lost Wing Commander Douglas Bader himself. Fortunately I baled out and received help from the French, which ultimately enabled me to escape over the Pyrenees. Whilst I was hiding on a farm in the Pas-de-Calais, I was visited by a British agent, Sydney Bowen, who was from an escape organisation based in Marseille. He asked me why more Spitfires were crashing in France than Me 109s. I had no answer for him.

Owing to the intercepts of German communications by ULTRA, the highest level of command in England was aware of actual German losses, but to make this public knowledge would have meant a massive morale problem. Indeed, after the Nazi invasion of Russia, the RAF's 'Non-Stop Offensive' was increased as a gesture of support towards Stalin. Although the intention was to hold German units on the Channel coast and thus prevent them from going east, JG2 and JG26, the two fighter groups entrusted with defending the *Kanalfront* neither went to Russia nor were reinforced.

On December 7th, 1941, the USA entered the war against the Axis powers when Japan executed a surprise air attack on the American fleet at Pearl Harbour. Soon afterwards American resources began arriving in Britain. On April 17th, 1942, General Ira Eaker led a formation of B17 'Flying Fortress' bombers to attack the Rouen-Sotteville marshalling yards. From that point onwards, Nazi Germany's fate was sealed.

A brief advantage enjoyed by the Germans during 1941/42 was provided by the advent of the radial-engined Focke-Wulf 190. Air Vice-Marshal Johnnie Johnson once gave me an informed view:-

Until we got the Spitfire Mk IX, the Germans always had a slight edge. The Me 109E was always slightly superior to the Spitfire Mk IA because of the 20 mm cannons and fuel injection. By comparison we had a First World War-type weapon in the 0.303 inch Browning machine-gun. The Me 109F was also slightly better than the Spitfire Mk V. Of course the FW190 then appeared and saw everybody off. It drove us back to the coast. Our depth of penetration over France was far shorter in 1942, just because of the 190 menace. It was not until we got the Spitfire Mk IX that the balance tipped firmly in our favour.

By mid-1943, the tide had definitely turned. The situation in North Africa had been redefined, and RAF fighter pilots also flew over that continent with great skill and courage. No essay on RAF fighter pilots in World War Two would be complete without mention of Malta, the air battles over which Mediterranean island, according to some survivors, 'made the Battle of Britain seem like child's play'. Was it a coincidence, I wonder, that the same man in charge of the airborne defence of Malta was the same senior officer tasked with the defence of London and Southern England during 1940? His name was Air Vice-Marshal Sir Keith Park, and beyond doubt we, the free world, will always be in his debt.

By this time, the Allied fighter pilot's role was changing. On July 10th, 1943, the Allies began an amphibious landing on Sicily. Flight Lieutenant Ron Rayner:-

We started the long slog up the western coast, flying patrols of Augusta and Catania, landing at the latter. From there we began escorting American Mitchell and Boston bombers, and I must say that their pilots were extremely brave. In addition to our escort work, we ourselves were attacking retreating Germans. On September 9th, the invasion of Italy was commenced, and our role was to support the army that was landing at Salerno. We patrolled the beaches, milling about with German aircraft attacking our ground forces, and whilst the navy shelled German positions. This went on until September 15th, by which time our bridgehead was secure and a landing strip had been created parallel to the beach. Although we could land at Salerno it was fraught with danger as not only were the Germans still shelling us but also the trajectory of our own artillery went across the airfield!

After a spell in hospital suffering from malaria, I returned to fly Spitfires with 72 Squadron for the remainder of the Italian campaign. We were largely engaged in ground attack against the German army, dive-bombing and strafing. We attacked convoys of their motor transport and armour. This entailed flying very low, and I once returned to base trailing a length of telegraph wire from my wingtip – the airfield cleared rapidly!

When I had been involved with the sweeps over France during 1941, I often wondered what good we were doing. Flying ground attack sorties in support of our army was different. You could see the effect of your shells on enemy vehicles and positions, and felt that you really were personally making a difference to our boys down there.

The experience gained during the successful landings on Sicily and Italy would prove invaluable for the liberation of France. Fighter pilots based in England were kept very busy during 1943 and 1944. Not only were innumerable bomber escort sorties flown, but also ground attack. By now the RAF had another Hawker fighter which excelled in this role: the Typhoon. This massive beast, capable of carrying bombs and rockets, and packing a mighty punch with four 20 mm cannons, roamed far and wide over enemy occupied territory blasting trains, tanks, motor transport and shipping. Mustangs and Spitfires too hunted the enemy both on the ground and in the air. The stage was now set for the final scene.

As purpose designed offensive fighters appeared, like the American Mustang, Thunderbolt and Lightning, it was ultimately possible to escort the bombers all the way to Berlin and back. The basis of the experience necessary to do so, however, had in fact been hard won by Fighter Command during 1941. Hans 'Peter' Wulff was a young *Leutnant* flying fighters in defence of Germany, who commented that:-

Eventually the Allied fighters were able to penetrate not only to Berlin, but also to our bases. These two factors made the situation hopeless, but we fought on.

On June 6th, 1944, the Allies successfully landed on the beaches of Normandy in one of the greatest feats of arms ever seen. The *Luftwaffe*, however, put in only a token appearance. Pilot Officer Tony Minchin, a Mustang pilot with 122 Squadron, remembers the invasion as 'an anti-climax from the aerial point of view'. It was nevertheless an awesome experience, as Flight Lieutenant Bob Beardsley DFC told newspaper reporters shortly after landing from a D-Day sortie:-

The sky over the target was absolutely packed with aircraft. Fighters and bombers seemed to fill the air flying wing-tip to wing-tip. From above (we fighter pilots) could see the bombs go down. The whole target area was a mass of flames. It was both an impressive and terrifying sight, and I for one was glad that I was not a German soldier.

When the bombers turned for home they left a belt of black smoke two miles wide by nine miles long, and from the reflection through the smoke it seemed as if the earth itself was on fire beneath.

A Norwegian Wing Leader added:-

Looking down on the target area was like looking down into hell.

The invasion heralded a new, nomadic existence for many Fighter Command squadrons. Johnnie Johnson remembered:-

Yes, it was a great time. We were soon able to land in France and operate our Spitfires from temporary airstrips, thus keeping on the move and in direct support of the army. It was very exciting.

On June 25th, 1944, Tony Minchin wrote in his diary:-

Yesterday the lads knocked down an FW190 and landed on an airstrip in Normandy. Today we all took off for our new airstrip, B7, near Martragny.

Our base is practically on the Caen-Bayeux road and our tents are pitched in an apple orchard. The natives seem apathetic and unmoved and probably don't care whether it is us or the Germans who are there. Being in the country seems to have left them largely untouched by the Occupation.

Also flying in defence of the Reich, the *Luftwaffe* was hopelessly outnumbered over France, and air-to-air combat lacked frequency and tempo as the whole emphasis shifted almost entirely to ground attack. There were exceptions, however, as Tony Minchin recorded on July 5th:-

Armed recce in the afternoon. Spotted a lone aircraft tucking in and out of broken cloud. We crept up behind and underneath him and saw that it was an Me 109G. Jimmy Talalla attacked but overshot and found himself right alongside the Hun who had an ace-of-spades emblem on his engine cowling. He then half-rolled and dived vertically to the deck. I thought that he would never pull out, but he did, just above the trees. Then followed a chase at zero feet. He used every contour of the land, going under telegraph wires etc, making it a difficult deflection shot. Alan and Jimmy took pots at him, but I was behind and as he rose slightly over a small hill I gave him a five second burst from 300 yards. Strikes appeared all over him and he went smack into the deck at 300 mph.

Tony's entry of July 30th relates a more typical sortie:-

Off dive-bombing a close support target SE of Caumont. Took off for the first time with 1000 pound bomb under each wing. Apart from feeling like a pregnant pig on take-off, the aircraft behaved quite well, although I built up to 500 mph in the dive. Fighter sweep in the evening, marshalling yards at Louye hit with good results.

That fighter pilots have a certain and enviable style is indicated by Tony's diary on August 8th:-

Another armed recce this morning – some flak. In the evening we had a real party, inviting 50 army nurses from just outside Bayeux. Planes had been flown to England to bring back lobster, ham, pies, trifle, beer and spirits. A platform was erected outside the Mess tent and a five-piece band played. It was a great success!

On August 7th, 1944, Hitler counter-attacked against the Allies at Mortain, but the Canadians unleashed Operation Totalize against Falaise, towards which Montgomery also moved. Patton swung round through France and turned north, the German army being trapped between two pincers. The gap, at Falaise, remained open, and as the Germans attempted to retreat across the Seine, the most incredible enemy targets presented themselves. The floor of the valley was alive with German soldiers cycling, marching and running, columns of horse-drawn transport, motor transport and armour. The Trun-Chambois road became a killing ground, known as both the 'Shambles' or 'Corridor of Death'. Aircraft of both the 2nd Tactical Air Force and the IXth American Air Force strafed the enemy until it was too dark to see. From dawn onwards on the following day, the Allied fighter-bombers hammered away, achieving complete panic amongst the enemy. The RAF's Typhoon squadrons flew a total of 294 sorties in just over eight hours, claiming the destruction of 84 tanks as 'flamers', 35 as 'smokers', and a further 21 damaged along with numerous motor vehicles. In response, just three 'Tiffies' were lost. The deployment of Typhoons was both timely and decisive, as although fighting remained bitter on the ground, large-scale attacks by *panzer* divisions were not renewed.

Amongst the Typhoon pilots engaged at Falaise was Pilot Officer John Thould of 263 Squadron. His log book records many sorties against the German columns, including the following:-

August 7th: RP Attack of gun and mortar positions west of Thury-Harcourt. Well plastered with RP and cannon.

August 10th: RP Attack on panzer HQ near Falaise. Lots of flak, chateau still burning from 'B' Flight's attack five hours previously.

August 26th: Mac and I got a poor bloke on a motor bike!

At the time, Flying Officer Peter Taylor was flying Mustangs with 65 Squadron, and his log book entries on August 19th, reflect the numbers of Allied aircraft in the air:-

Forcing on with big strafe. Sifta Section dive-bombed, not so dusty but too many Spitfires.

Same again but area getting clapped. Too many 'Tiffies' and too few trucks.

Although elements of the German army escaped the slaughter at Falaise to escape across the Seine and into the crumbling Reich, the Allies maintained the momentum. Bitter fighting still lay ahead as the Germans defended their homeland, but with the western Allies advancing ever eastwards, and with the Russians rolling up the eastern front, the fate of Nazi Germany was even more inevitable. On December 16th, 1944, Hitler launched his last major counter-attack against the West, the so-called Battle of the Bulge. On New Year's Day 1945, the Luftwaffe made its last attack: Operation Bodenplatte. Whilst their enemy recovered from the night before, German aircraft strafed and bombed Allied air bases on the continent. Although to some extent successful, not even this desperate surprise attack could have any bearing on the war's outcome.

On May 8th, 1945, the war in Europe was officially declared over and an Allied victory. Hitler's evil empire had been broken at last amid the destruction, misery and slaughter that he himself had unleashed upon the world in 1939.

After the surrender of Japan came the long process of demobilisation. This did not occur overnight, however, as Peter Taylor's logbook indicates:-

March 10th, 1946: Spitfire Mk XXI, LA282. Last dice with Issac Newton.

Some fighter pilots remained in the peacetime RAF, others tried, as best they could, to put the war behind them. Ron Rayner, for example, returned home to family life and a completely new set of commitments and priorities. A jeweller, it was always difficult to imagine this softly spoken and creative gentleman strafing and dive-bombing his way up Italy. Nevertheless, the past was always there, as Ron told me:-

There is not a day gone by that I have not thought about the war. About what we did, what we had to do.

William Walker, a Spitfire pilot who survived being shot down by the German 'ace' Major Werner Mölders during the Battle of Britain, puts it another way:-

The war would have been the most incredibly exciting and exhilarating time if no one had got killed. It has never ceased to amaze me how the skilled and experienced chaps often seemed to get killed whilst the hams and amateurs like me survived.

Who decides who lives and dies?

Regarding the casualties, all, without exception, were intelligent and fit young men, their potential proven by the successful careers, in both the services and many other walks of life, enjoyed by the survivors. Without a doubt, the world has been a poorer place for their passing.

Surviving Second World War fighter pilots today make fascinating companions. All are now elderly and some, by their own admission, struggle to recall what they had for breakfast. All, however, seem to recall with great pride and clarity when they flew Spitfires, or whatever. Most, with only a couple of notable exceptions, are modest men who insist that the next man's story is more interesting.

In November 1998, I was involved in a short documentary made by Carlton Television for the Central region. One of the scenes involved Ron Rayner and Battle of Britain Spitfire pilot Ken Wilkinson looking over artefacts from Spitfires recovered by the former Malvern Spitfire Team. As the camera's eye focussed on the two veterans, Ken put his arm around Ron and, with a twinkle in his eye, said:-

If you were a fighter pilot you were considered to be a cocky bugger, top buttons undone and all that. We definitely thought that we were a cut above the rest!

No further comment required!

Dilip Sarkar, Worcester, March 2001

Fighter Pilot:
The Photographic Kaleidoscope

Posing with a Hawker Fury biplane during training are three fledgling fighter pilots. The only pilot identified is at left, Pilot Officer Jack Hamar who joined 151 Squadron at North Weald in 1939. Equipped with Hurricanes, 151 later fought during the French campaign and the first stage of the Battle of Britain. Having destroyed six enemy aircraft and probably destroyed six more, Hamar was killed on July 24th, 1940, in a tragic flying accident at North Weald. News of his DFC award had, unbeknown to the unfortunate pilot, been received that very day.

Another Hurricane squadron that served in France during 1940, was 607 'County of Durham' Squadron, an Auxiliary unit. These pilots of that squadron are pictured at Usworth immediately before their departure for France, and are from left to right: Harry Radcliffe, Robert Pumphrey, Jim Bazin, 'Humph' Humpherson, unknown, Dudley Craig, Joe Kyall, Alan Glover and Tony 'Nit' Whitty. Note the mixture of flying clothing, including pre-war black flying suits.

Five Spitfire pilots of 74 'Tiger' Squadron pictured at a muddy Gravesend airfield during the spring of 1941: Pilot Officer HRG Poulton, Flight Lieutenant JC Freeborn DFC, Flying Officer HC Baker, Flying Officer Woods and Pilot Officer EA Mould. All except Woods were survivors of the Battle of Britain, of the group only Mould would not survive the war. His grave can be found at Brookwood Military Cemetery.

By 1941, the Spitfire had started to replace the Hurricane in front line use. This Hurricane belonged to 504 'City of Nottingham' Squadron and was photographed by Battle of Britain survivor Sergeant BM 'Mike' Bush at Exeter. In October, the Squadron received Spitfire Mk IIAs. This really is a great snapshot of a rather war weary aircraft.

During the Battle of Britain, squadrons were cleverly rotated from the combat zone in the south to rest and re-fit in northern England. This ensured that there were always effective operational squadrons available in southern England. Squadrons in the north were used as an extension of the OTU process, amongst them 65 'East India' Squadron. This picture was taken at Kirton in March 1941, and shows (from left, rear row): P/O Rathie, Sgt Hewlett (KIA Dec 1942), Sgt Johnson (POW Oct 1941), Sgt Mitchell (KIA June 1944), P/O MacPherson (MIA, Oct 1941). Sitting: Flt Lt

Grant (later AVM, died 1987), Sgt Rose (KIA May 1941), Sgt Oldnall (KIA Dec 1941), Sgt Stillwell & Sgt Foulger.

Sergeant J. Johnson pictured at right with an unknown 65 Squadron pilot. The aircraft is 'YT-B' and appears to have the Polish chequered square beneath the cockpit. Sadly Johnson remained affected by his experiences in captivity and committed suicide in 1967.

A well-known press photograph taken at Tangmere on a foggy afternoon in February 1941. The pilots are in 'best blue' because just as the press arrived, flying having been 'scrubbed', according to the late Ron Stillwell they were 'just about to set off on a sweep of the local pubs!' From left to right: Sgt Orchard (killed the next day), Sgt Chalmers, Fg Off Finucane DFC (MIA 1942), Fg Off Wigg (died 1979), Sgt Rose (KIA 1941), Sgt Mitchell (KIA 1944).

Amongst those pilots pictured in the preceding famous 65 Squadron photograph is Hugh Chalmers, who missed qualifying as one of the Few by a matter of days. Note that in this photograph, taken at Kirton in 1941, Hugh is wearing non-regulation sheepskin gloves.

Retiring from the RAF as a Flight Lieutenant in 1946, Hugh's working life was as a PE teacher. He is pictured here at the launch of my fifth book, A Few of the Many, in which his story was featured.

A 65 'East India' Squadron Spitfire Mk IIA pictured at Tangmere during early 1941.

The story of Sergeant Peter Rose is a tragic one. Having transferred from 65 Squadron when based at Kirton in April 1941, Peter joined No 1 PRU at Benson. On May 3rd, his Spitfire failed to return from a sortie to photograph the Ruhr valley. Forced to abandon R6805 due to an inexplicable engine fire, his parachute was damaged when hit by debris when the aircraft exploded.

Peter Rose caused problems for the Germans in death. Over 1,000 Belgians turned out to his funeral, creating a potentially serious public order problem for the Germans. His burial in the local churchyard having been prohibited by the Germans, Rose was by day buried near his crash site. By night, villagers exhumed his coffin in secret and bravely re-buried the gallant young pilot in the churchyard. After the war both the Rose family and villagers protested at the CWGC's intention to move the body to a communal military cemetery. 'People Power' won the day, so the grave of Sergeant Peter Rose can still be found in the village of Soumagne, near Liege, in Belgium.

Robert Harold 'Jack' Strang received his flying brevet with the RNZAF in November 1939. By May 1940, he was completing his service flying training in England with the RAF, joining 65 Squadron at Turnhouse on September 2nd, 1940. Later becoming a flight commander with the all-New Zealand 485 Squadron, by January 25th, 1942, Strang had made 104 flights in 18 months. Operational flights numbered 67: 18 sweeps, three 'scrambles', 30 bomber escort sorties, five ASR patrols and eight convoy protection sorties. On that fateful day, however, Flight Lieutenant Strang fell victim to oxygen system failure whilst on patrol high over the English Channel. His Spitfire crashed into the sea off Dover, another pilot reported 'Missing'.

'Missing in Action' would be the fate of many fine young men between 1939-45. Also amongst them was Pilot Officer Victor Lowson from Dundee. On July 21st, 1942, 65 Squadron participated in a 'Debden Wing mass Rhubarb'. Twelve Spitfires strafed various targets at Zeebrugge, but Lowson's aircraft was hit by machine-gun fire shortly after crossing the coast. Two miles out to sea he prepared to bale out but his aircraft suddenly plunged into the sea. Although his friend, Warrant Officer Ron Stillwell DFM, circled the spot several times, nothing was ever seen of Lowson again.

On November 26th, 1940, Vic Lowson was on patrol but became separated from his section in fading light. With a u/s R/T, and faced with no other alternative, he baled out. Any person whose life was saved by an Irvin parachute was illegible for membership of the 'Caterpillar Club'. Each member was awarded a tiny gold caterpillar brooch, red eyes indicating that the wearer had taken to his parachute over land, green eyes meant over the sea. This example, with red eyes, once belonged to Vic Lowson and relates to his escapade in November 1940.

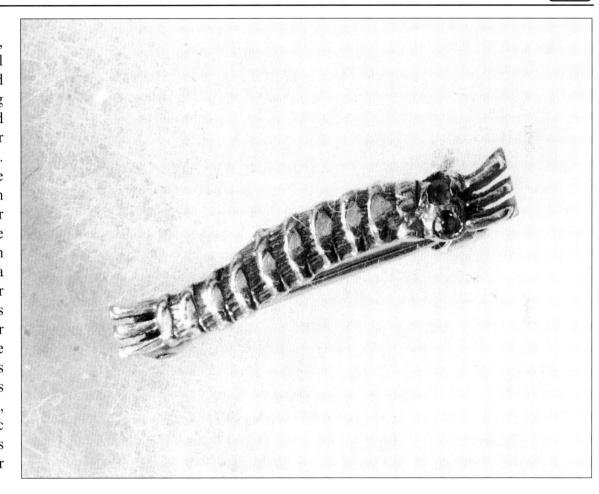

Flight Lieutenant John Stenton's career was an interesting one given that he joined the RAF as a mere 'Aircrafthand' in 1931. In 1933, he remustered as a wireless operator under training, and again in 1937 as a pilot. Unfortunately a road accident put a temporary halt to his flying training, but this he successfully completed in August 1940. He then learnt to fly Spitfires before being posted to fly Defiant night-fighters with 256 Squadron at Pembrey. After a spell instructing, Stenton flew Spitfires with 222 Squadron, but he then volunteered to fly catapult Hurricanes with the Merchant Ship Fighter Unit. Perhaps fortunately the unit disbanded before Stenton went to sea. Flight Lieutenant Stenton then flew Hurricanes briefly with 131 Squadron before a posting to HQ RAF Burma. On June 1st, 1945, he went 'missing' whilst flying an Expeditor, bound for Kinmagon. The wreck of Stenton's aircraft was never found, despite extensive search operations in the jungle, which went on until 1956. His name can be found on the Singapore War Memorial.

The album of Hornchurch & 41 Squadron Battle of Britain veteran Squadron Leader Bob Beardsley DFC is a veritable treasure trove, and the 14 photographs that follow are therefrom. Bob took this snapshot of Pilot Officer JJ 'Chris' Le Roux, a South African, at Catterick in early 1941. Le Roux became an 'ace' with 18 confirmed victories, but went 'missing' on a routine flight from Normandy to England in 1944. Shortly before his presumed death, Le Roux had strafed a German staff car in Normandy. It was later believed that the wounded occupants included none other than Feldmarschall Erwin Rommel.

Sergeant Mitchell, of 41 Squadron, photographed at Catterick in 1941. Having destroyed an Me 109F on August 7th, 1941, 'Mitch' would himself be reported 'missing' in due course.

One of 41 Squadron's accomplished NCO pilots during the Battle of Britain period was Frank Usmar, pictured here at 'Readiness', Catterick, 1941. His nickname was 'ITMA', short for the popular Tommy Handley show 'It's That Man Again!'

Bob Beardsley himself at 'Readiness', Catterick, 1941.

Another Catterick shot and another replacement pilot: Sergeant Len Thorne.

The Likely Lads? 41 Squadron (informal!) group, Catterick 1941. Bob's caption reads: 'ITMA, Johnny, George, Tom, Sticky & Ray'.

Bob snapped this photograph of Sergeant Glew whilst standing on the top of a blast pen. Glew's nickname was inevitably 'Sticky'!

'Sticky' Glew again.

Flight Lieutenant Pat Meagher also snapped at 'Readiness'. A successful fighter pilot, in 1943, Meagher was posted to the Far East. Flying Beaufighters, he destroyed numerous Japanese aircraft, his final score being nine destroyed, two probables and one damaged. He finished the war as a Group Captain awarded both the DSO and DFC.

41 Squadron pilot Harry Fowler, another post-Battle of Britain replacement.

'Tom Hindle & Sticky'.

41 Squadron 'Readiness' group at Catterick, Sergeant Frank Usmar at right.

Also at Catterick, Sergeants Bob
Beardsley, 'Mitch' Mitchell and
Frank Usmar.

The final picture in Bob's Catterick sequence shows Sergeant Ron 'Cloudy' Rayner. A grammar school boy, when Ron volunteered for aircrew duties he took with him a letter of recommendation from his maths teacher.

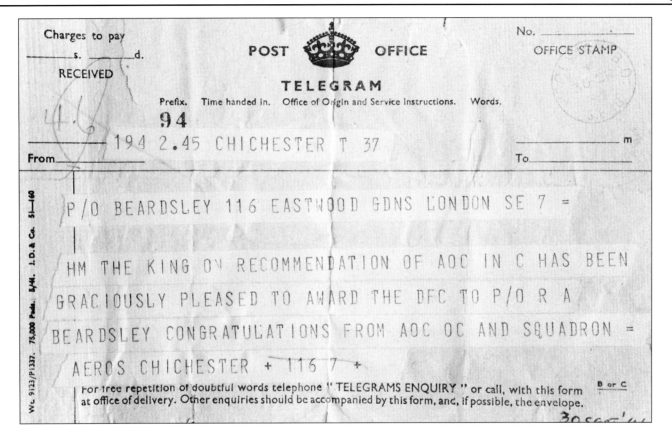

The telegram received by Pilot Officer Bob Beardsley informing of his DFC award, September 30th, 1941.

Another keen photographer was Peter Howard-Williams, who was quite a character! Having first flown with 19 Squadron, Peter later joined 118 Squadron at Ibsley, where this snapshot was taken in early 1941, of him posing with his Spitfire Mk IIA. Note the parachute on the wingtip.

On February 2ⁿᵈ, 1942, Flight Lieutenant Howard-Williams DFC and Pilot Officer Ted Ames flew 'Rhubarb 87', an attack against the alcohol distillery at Éroudeville. Near the French coast, the two Spitfires were 'bounced' by Me 109s of JG2. Ames disappeared over the sea, and Peter's Spitfire, AD209, was hit hard by cannon shells. Dodging into cloud, Peter managed to nurse his Spitfire back to England where he managed to land normally at Ibsley. Here a rather shaken Peter is snapped next to AD209.

Flight Lieutenant Peter Howard-Williams DFC (right) and an unknown pilot pose with 118 Squadron's scoreboard.

The morale raising film about RJ Mitchell and the creation of his Spitfire, The First of the Few starred Leslie Howard and David Niven. Filmed at Ibsley, the pilots of 118 and 501 Squadrons supplied the pilots and Spitfires. This snapshot, taken with his own camera, shows Peter Howard-Williams (centre) in conversation with Flying Officer John Robson and Leslie Howard.

Also believed to have been taken by Peter during the making of the film, here we have Flight Sergeant Lewis, NCO in charge of 'A' Flight's groundcrew, with Pilot Officer Walter Milne. The Spitfire belonged to 501 Squadron.

An unknown Pilot Officer of 118 Squadron snapped at Ibsley by Peter. Sadly Wing Commander Howard-Williams died in 1993, before our work to caption his many photographs was complete.

Although the Hurricane began to be replaced as a day-fighter by Spitfires after the Battle of Britain, Camm's fighter was part of Britain's nocturnal front line. No 87 Squadron, for example, had flown in the defence of the West Country by day during the summer and autumn of 1940, but from November 1940 onwards was often used at night. Based at St Mary's on the Scilly Isles, here we have Pilot Officer Watson, Sergeant Thorogood, unknown, Squadron Leader Gleed, Pilot Officer Tait and Flight Lieutenant (Roddy) Rayner.

From Squadron Leader Laurence Thorogood's personal album, one of 87 Squadron's 'Black Beasts' in 1941.

Line-up of 87 Squadron Hurricanes at Charmy Down, 1941. Each Hurricane is equipped with four 20 mm cannon. Many of these aircraft were presented by overseas provinces.

Maintenance work on an 87 Squadron Hurricane. Note the camouflage netting.

Spitfires too were pressed into the nocturnal role during the night blitz of 1941, No 19 Squadron based at Fowlmere in the Duxford Sector making numerous night patrols in an attempt to protect the industrial Midlands. This shows the interior of the pilots' hut at Fowlmere early during 1941. At centre is Flight Lieutenant Jack 'Farmer' Lawson DFC.

So captioned 'The mind of a pilot' in the personal album of former 19 Squadron pilot Wing Commander David Cox DFC.

Shooting game on the wing was an excellent means of practice, and many fighter pilots pursued the sport when the opportunity arose. Here 19 Squadron's Flight Lieutenant Lawson and Sergeant Cox examine a kill by Flight Lieutenant Wallace 'Jock' Cunningham DFC.

On August 28th, 1941, 19 Squadron was involved in an ill-conceived raid against enemy shipping off Rotterdam. Amongst the casualties was Flight Lieutenant Cunningham, a flight commander and most experienced pilot, who was brought down by anti-aircraft fire. Having crash-landed his Spitfire on a beach 'Jock' was captured. He is pictured here at second right whilst in the 'bag'. The two pilots to his right are also of 19 Squadron, Pilot Officers Andrews and Cowley.

Sadly Lawson, by then CO, was shot down by an Me 109 of JG53 and disappeared into the North Sea. Here he is pictured in the 'office' of Spitfire P7849, presented by the Belfast Telegraph.

Amongst Fighter Command's most notable personalities was the legless fighter pilot Douglas Bader. In March 1941, Wing Commander Bader was given the Tangmere Wing, and immediately set about a busy schedule of offensive operations. He led at the head of 616 Squadron, flying from what is now Goodwood Motor Racing Circuit. He is pictured here, the right of the two men with pipes, outside the 616 pilots' hut during the summer of 1941. Also included are, from left to right: Flight Lieutenant Denys Gillam (visiting), Sgt McCairns, Plt Off Heppell, Sgt West, Sgt Brewer, Squadron Clerk, Plt Off Johnson. The other pilot smoking a pipe is Squadron Leader Burton, the CO of 616.

Squadron Leader HF 'Billy' Burton DFC walks in at Goodwood after a sweep during the summer of 1941. Note that he is wearing a German lifejacket. Sadly Burton was amongst a number of experienced RAF officers shot down into the Bay of Biscay whilst travelling in an unarmed Hudson back to North Africa on June 3rd, 1943. His name can also be found amongst the 'Missing'.

Another star of the Tangmere Wing, and close friend of Wing Commander Bader: Squadron Leader Stan Turner DFC, CO of 145 Squadron. Turner, a Canadian, had previously flown with Bader in 242 Squadron during the Battle of Britain. An 'ace' Turner died in 1985. He was one of the few characters referred to by their actual names in the Bader film Reach for the Sky.

Sergeant Peter Ward-Smith of the Tangmere Wing's 610 Squadron. He was shot down and captured on July 10th, 1941.

This really is an amazing photograph, so study closely! This Spitfire is P7666, Manxman, which became Wing Commander Bader's personal aircraft for most of the time that he commanded the Tangmere Wing. A colour Kodak cine-gun camera is being fitted to the aircraft, hence the occasion having been recorded by RAF photographer Norman Jenkins. Of greater interest, however, is the noseart, clearly visible beneath the aircraft's exhaust stubs. This shows Hitler receiving a kick up the backside by an RAF flying boot, similar to that

painted on Bader's Battle of Britain Hurricane. Despite the fact that this picture was first published in my Bader's Tangmere Spitfires (PSL, 1996), this essential detail remains missing from artwork concerning this Spitfire.

A close-up of a combat cine camera as fitted to a Spitfire, but this is not Wing Commander Bader's aircraft. The camera was synchronised to shoot simultaneously with the aircraft's guns, thus recording results.

Whilst at Goodwood watching the camera being fitted, Norman also snapped this section of Spitfires taking off. Unfortunately we do not know the exact date, but it would certainly be interesting to know which pilots were involved, what their sortie was and, indeed, their fate.

Alan Smith was a Sergeant-Pilot in the VR who joined 616 Squadron after the Battle of Britain. When Wing Commander Bader told him to fly as his Number Two, the astonished Smith considered it akin to 'being told to keep an eye on heaven'! Although Smith belonged to 616, this Spitfire was on charge with 610 Squadron (DW).

Sergeant Smith with the 616 Squadron Intelligence Officer, Flying Officer 'Spy' Gibbs. Smith later flew with distinction over Malta, and after the war received a knighthood.

616 Squadron pilots snapped by Pilot Officer Johnnie Johnson posing with the Wing Commander's Spitfire. Lying on the cowling is Sergeant West, who died recently in New Zealand, Sergeant Brewer points out the Hitler motif, Sergeant SWR 'Thug' Mabbett, and Pilot Officer 'Nip' Hepple (who died in 1986).

Also snapped by Pilot Officer Johnson, Sergeant Syd Mabbett from Cheltenham. Whilst flying as wingman to Johnson, on July 21st, 1941, Mabbett was shot down near St Omer by Unteroffizier Dietze of 2/JG26.

754550

SJT.S.W.R.MABBETT
R.A.F.

21.7.41

So impressed were the Germans by the mortally wounded Mabbett's effort to successfully force-land his Spitfire, that they buried him with full military honours at Longuenesse Military Cemetery, St Omer. This is the original wooden marker photographed by the Red Cross during the war and sent home to the family.

On June 21st, 1941, the Tangmere Wing flew as Target Support for a 'Circus' to St Omer. During the return flight, 145 Squadron's Sergeant Frank Twitchett was attacked near the English coast by Oberleutnant Matzke of II/JG26. Although wounded and with a badly damaged Spitfire, Frank managed to escape and land safely back at Merston. Here Dave Horne, of 145's ground staff, pokes his head through the damaged rudder of P8341 (SO-J). This shows what serious damage just one 20 mm cannon shell could inflict.

August 9th, 1941, was a black day for the Tangmere Wing, as Wing Commander Bader failed to return from a sweep to St Omer. Although the circumstances of his demise have yet to be satisfactorily explained, we do know that 'Dogsbody' baled out, after some difficulty, and was captured by the Germans. Also captured that day was 616 Squadron stalwart Flight Lieutenant Lionel 'Buck' Casson, whose Spitfire was attacked whilst heading back to the French coast. This is 'Buck's' SpitfireW3458, photographed by the Germans at Marquise. The fire damage resulted from the pilot igniting the port-fire, carried to assist destruction in such circumstances.

*C*asson was shot down by Hauptmann Gerhard Schöpfel, Kommandeur of III/JG26. Now aged 88, he is still enjoying retirement in Germany.

Naturally the Germans had heard a great deal about Wing Commander Bader, the legless British 'ace'. The Kommodore of JG26, Oberstleutnant Adolf Galland, invited the captive Wing Commander to visit his Geschwaderstabstaffel (Group Staff Flight) at Audembert, near Calais. Bader met his German opponents and given a tour of the airfield. Wing Commander Bader is seen here accompanied by Galland (front row, left) and his officers.

Another casualty of the Non-Stop Offensive was Sergeant Clifford Jacka, an only son from Bournemouth. Flying Spitfire P8046, City of Worcester II, Jacka, of 234 Squadron, was shot down on August 26th, 1941, whilst strafing an enemy airfield near Cherbourg. Turning out to sea he managed to ditch his Spitfire, but sadly drowned.

Sergeant Jacka's grave in Cherbourg cemetery. In 1995, Ramrod Publications sponsored a plaque commemorating the two pilots killed flying the Worcester presentation Spitfires. Appropriately this was unveiled by Mr Peter Fox, who was not only flying with Sergeant Jacka when he was killed but who also had the unenviable task of personally informing the unfortunate pilot's parents.

Ready to go! A Polish pilot, Flying Officer Stanislaw Wandzilak of 308 'City of Krakow' Squadron, prepares to take off from RAF Northolt.

Safely home: a Polish Spitfire lands at Northolt after a sweep.

Pilot Officer Stanislaw Wielgus of 308 Squadron. An experienced pilot, after Poland surrendered he flew with the French Air Force. When France fell, together with Witold Retinger, Wielgus escaped to England in a French bomber. On July 12th, 1941, whilst 308 Squadron was a part of the Northolt Wing, Wielgus failed to return from a 'Circus' to Hazebrouck. The following day, amidst torrential rain and rolling thunder, the 31-year old Pole's broken body was washed up on the south coast. Consequently he was buried by his Squadron with full military honours at Northwood Military Cemetery, where his grave can be found today. This photograph was taken in Poland before the war (note PAF insignia, including the Polish eagle flying badge). The reverse is inscribed 'With affectionate remembrances' by Stanislaw Wandzilak.

The loss of Pilot Officer Wielgus was most keenly felt by fellow 308 Squadron pilot, Bruno Kudrewicz. The pair shared Room 13 together.

Many Czechs also flew with the RAF during World War Two. These pilots are from the Czech 310 Squadron, pictured at Duxford shortly after the Battle of Britain. The pilot at right is clearly explaining how his last kill was achieved!

Atmospheric snapshot of 310 Squadron Spitfire Mk V.

As indicated by AVM Johnson in my Introduction, the use of 20 mm cannon by the Germans early in the war provided a big advantage. After initial problems the RAF followed suit, however. Here armourers at Biggin Hill in 1941, load 20 mm shells into an ammunition drum.

An armourer poses at Biggin Hill with a 20 mm cannon, made by Hispano Suiza. The cannon weighed some 96 pounds and was seven feet long. Only the section from the man's hand upwards to the barrel's end protruded from the wing.

Not all damage to operational aircraft was caused by enemy action. This Spitfire of 610 Squadron, for example, was damaged during a flying accident. Sergeants Joe Doley and Peter Horner ponder the pilot's apparently miraculous escape at Acklington.

Although this Spitfire is believed to be from 74 Squadron at Biggin Hill, and the incident sometime during 1941, no other details are known. Given that this was obviously a safe and controlled forced-landing one assumes that the pilot survived. Is he, I wonder, either of the two pilots flanking the two 'erks'? If so, who was he?

The next four photographs are from the personal album of Air Commodore Peter Brothers DSO DFC*, Deputy Chairman of the Battle of Britain Fighter Association, and date from his leadership of 457 (Australian) Squadron. Here a Spitfire Mk IIA safely takes off.

Formation of 457 Squadron Spitfires in close formation, snapped by the CO!

The Spitfires to the CO's left. The photograph was taken over the Isle of Man in 1941.

This snap by Pete Brothers of a crash landed 457 Squadron Spitfire is interesting as it clearly shows the reduction gearing between the De Havilland airscrew and Rolls-Royce Merlin engine. The inverted 'V' of the mighty Merlin can also be seen.

The FW190 scourge caused so many casualties that a commando raid was planned with the objective of stealing a 'Butcher Bird' from France. This became unnecessary when on June 23rd, 1942, Oberleutnant Armin Faber of Stab III/JG2 landed by mistake at Pembrey in South Wales. After combat near Start Point, Faber mistook the Bristol Channel for the English Channel and thus delivered an intact 190 to the RAF. Amongst the Spitfire pilots who flew to Pembrey the following day to examine Faber's exceptional fighter was Flight Lieutenant THD Drinkwater of 234 Squadron. Pictured here, Drinkwater took numerous snaps of the 190.

Close-up by Drinkwater of Faber's 190 which clearly shows the cockerel's head of III/JG2. This arose from a play on words, the Gruppenkommandeur's name – Hahn – also meaning cockerel.

Oberleutnant Armin Faber himself, pictured at Pembrey. He was escorted to RAF Fairwood Common and was a guest of the Officers' Mess there for two days before being sent to London for interrogation.

At Pembrey, 'Drink' also snapped some of his fellow pilots, although unfortunately he has not recorded their identities (this being a common enough feature, as we shall see). This is possibly Squadron Leader MV Blake.

Our only clue with the identity of this Spitfire pilot is 'Canadian pilot'. The aircraft belongs to 234 Squadron, the date June 1942. 'Daphne' appears to be written beneath the windscreen.

Sensibly, trainee RAF pilots were sent to Canada and the USA where they were taught to fly, returning to the UK for conversion to operational type. This photograph, taken in the USA, includes (extreme right) Sergeant Donald Machin, from Lancashire. Whilst training on Spitfires with 52 OTU at Aston Down in Gloucestershire, on July 23rd, 1942, Machin crashed into the River Severn off Sudbrook, Gwent, and was killed.

Allan White Collection

Sergeant Jack Pierce of the RCAF was also killed when his 52 OTU Spitfire, R7135, crashed into the River Severn (February 2nd, 1942). The rate of attrition in training was high, and the UK is littered with the crashes of wartime aircraft lost in such circumstances.

Allan White Collection

George Lock came from the tiny village of Bronllys, near Brecon, so flying training in the USA opened up a whole new world. Here Sergeant Lock is pictured posing with a belt of bullets during a live firing exercise. The picture is captioned in his album 'Come a shooting, Bud!'.

Sergeants Lock & Kelly proudly wearing both the RAF flying brevet and USAAC pilot's badge after their 'Wings Parade' in the USA.

Having been trained on Beaufighters back in the UK, Sergeant Lock was posted to the Telecommunications Flying Unit at RAF Defford in Worcestershire, this unit providing aircraft for the 'boffins' at nearby Malvern's Telecommunications Research Establishment. There Lock had the opportunity to fly various types of aircraft, including Spitfire X4918. On February 26th, 1943, he took off in that Spitfire but collided with a Tiger Moth biplane from 2 EFTS Worcester. The 21-year old Welshman was killed, the Australian 'Tiggie' pilot, Sergeant JFC MacPherson, survived (only to be killed in another collision six months later). X4918 crashed at Park Farm, Pirton, and this is the oil filler cover as *recovered by the former Malvern Spitfire Team in 1993.*

Returning now to operations, another snapshot by Peter Howard-Williams, this time of a Spitfire Mk V of 118 Squadron at Ibsley. From left to right: Vanstae, Jones, Kerr. On wing: Ted Ames ('Missing' February 2nd, 1942) and Don Claxton (also 'Missing', 1942). The name 'Joe' is written on the cannon's barrel, the end of which is protected by a rubber sleeve.

Another Pole who fought valiantly throughout the war was Flight Lieutenant Kazek Budzik. Having joined 308 Squadron at Northolt in 1941, Budzik flew without a break and participated in D-Day and the ill-fated Arnhem operation of 1944. He is pictured here on October 29th, 1944, with his Spitfire Mk IX, bombed up and ready to go. A few minutes later he was shot down by light flak whilst attacking the Breda/Dortrecht bridge in Holland. Crash-landing 'ZF-A', he was back in action just two days later.

After the war, Kazek and his Polish wife, Helen, settled in Nottingham where he became a bus driver and raised a family. A real 'live wire', and one of the most energetic men that I have ever met, he nimbly leapt into the cockpit of an RAF Exhibition Flight Spitfire Mk XVI on display at the launch of my 'The Invisible Thread'. The event was held at the Abbey Hotel, Great Malvern, in September 1992.

Another old friend, but sadly no longer with us, is Flight Lieutenant HRG Poulton DFC. One of the Few, Bob and I came into contact many years ago because he had flown Spitfire P8047 The Malverns. His photograph album was impressive, the first that I saw in fact. This and the next 10 photographs are from it. In this snapshot, Bob poses with his 64 Squadron Spitfire Mk IX at Kenley.

The CO of 64 Squadron at that time, the Belgian Squadron Leader Michel Donnet DFC.

A contemporary of Bob's, with whom he flew in both 611 and 64 Squadrons, was the New Zealander 'ace' Bill Crawford-Compton. Bob has snapped him here with his 64 Squadron Spitfire Mk IX at Kenley in 1943. The nose art is of interest, The Magic Carpet.

Another 'ace' in 64 Squadron was the Rhodesian John Plagis. Very successful over Malta, although this picture was found in Bob's album it would appear to have been taken on the 'The George Cross Island'.

This is believed to be the American Elmer Draper, but no caption exists.

The Yanks are here! The occasion is unknown, but American aircrew are obviously visiting 64 Squadron at Kenley.

Pilots of 64 Squadron, snapped by Bob, pose with the Americans. John Plagis in foreground.

Bob Poulton pictured at Kenley, sitting on a Spitfire auxiliary fuel tank. These devices extended the aircraft's range and could be jettisoned when fuel therefrom was exhausted.

Two happy pilots of 64 Squadron. What became of them, I wonder?

Captioned simply 'Flying Officer Patterson', no other details are given.

Fighter squadron: 611 Squadron pictured at Kenley in 1942. The trophies are from a Ju 88 shot down over Wales during 1940 by Pilot Officer Dennis Adams.

74. SQDN's GREMLIN.

The 'Gremlin' was blamed for all inexplicable technical faults. This is 74 Squadron's!

'Ousting the Gremlin' seems to have been a good excuse for a party!

David Cox was the first NCO VR pilot posted to 19 Squadron in 1940. After the Battle of Britain he continued to enjoy success, going out to the desert with 72 Squadron in 1942. Here Flight Lieutenant Cox is pictured (seated) with his desert Spitfire, RN-B. Pat is David's wife, now of 60 years, and all of his Spitfires were named after her.

Squadron Leader Bobby Oxspring DFC, CO of 72 Squadron and also a successful fighter pilot from 1940 onwards, congratulates his flight commander, Flight Lieutenant Cox, on the award of his DFC, 1943. Note that both pilots are wearing service revolvers.

Peter Taylor listens whilst a fellow 65 Squadron pilot describes his latest success, 1943.

Royal pilot: Prince Bernhardt of the Netherlands is shown a Spitfire. His Royal Highness went on to become a Spitfire pilot himself.

Flight Lieutenant Ron Rayner DFC, who fought with 41, 43 and 72 Squadrons between 1941-45.

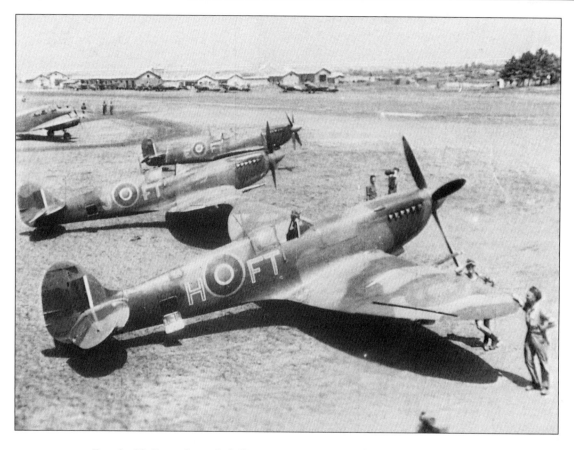

Ron's 43 Squadron Spitfire, 'FT-J', pictured at Catania, Sicily.

Ron's 72 Squadron Spitfire at Ravenna, 1945. A flak shell came through the wing during a strafing attack. Had it done so just three inches to the left, Ron would have been killed. Here his groundcrew pose with the damaged aircraft. Having survived this brush with the Reaper, Ron lived until April 9th, 1999, by which time he had recently become a great-grandfather.

Although Douglas Bader eclipsed all others, he was not, in fact, the only legless fighter pilot in the RAF. Colin Hodgkinson also lost his legs in a flying accident, but, inspired by Bader, became a Spitfire pilot. By coincidence, Colin's 131 Squadron also flew from Tangmere, and Colin was also captured near St Omer! Having enjoyed retirement living in the South of France, 'Hoppy' died in 1997.

This and the next 15 photographs came from the personal album of Air Marshal Sir Denis Crowley-Milling (DCM), one of the Few who was a close friend of Sir Douglas Bader's, the pair having first flown together in 242 Squadron during 1940. This is a remarkable snapshot, showing DCM's 242 Squadron Hurricane on January 10th, 1941. The Squadron was preparing for the first 'Circus' operation, a raid against ammunition supplies in the Fôret de Guines.

'Tea & Wads', an essential part of pre-flight preparation. Also taken on January 10th, 1941.

A member of 242 Squadron's groundcrew sat in the cockpit of DCM's Hurricane Mk II. Note the 20 mm cannons and Welsh griffin emblem.

Soon after Wing Commander Bader arrived at Tangmere in 1941, DCM joined him there, becoming a flight commander with 610 Squadron. This is his Spitfire at Goodwood (then called Westhampnett).

The same Spitfire, DW-X, BL584.

On August 21st, 1941, DCM was shot down over France but evaded capture. Passed down the line by the Resistance, he eventually escaped over the Pyrenees and returned to the UK. This snapshot was taken whilst he was on the run, disguised as a French civilian.

Shortly after returning home, DCM was given command of 181 Squadron, which was forming and equipped with Typhoons. Here he is shown in an early 'Tiffie' with a 'car door' type cockpit. Again, Hitler comes in for some rough treatment!

DCM briefs his Typhoon pilots on an exercise. Given the 'Knights Crosses', some would appear to be the enemy!

DCM (centre, seated), with 181 Squadron's pilots and groundcrew.

The mighty Typhoon, bombed up and known as a 'Bombphoon'.

Typhoon being bombed up.

The armourers 'make what dreadful note of preparation' (with apologies to Shakespeare!).

The role of the WAAF on front line airfields is often overlooked. Here a WAAF drives the tractor. The aircraft being bombed up is DCM's, note the Squadron Leader's rank pennant.

DCM airborne. Note the black and white invasion stripes intended to assist aircraft recognition.

A fearsome sight for any German serviceman!

Safely home, DCM taxis in, bombs gone.

A contemporary of DCM's was Tom Pugh, who formed 182 Squadron, and would have become the first Typhoon Wing Leader if not for his death in action on August 2nd, 1943. Squadron Leader Tom Pugh DFC was lost when his aircraft exploded during a dive-bombing attack on Dieppe harbour. The post of Wing Leader was therefore filled by DCM. Tom was one of three brothers, all of whom were pilots. Sadly Pilot Officer Jack Pugh was also killed, in a Spitfire flying accident during 1940, but Bob, the youngest, survived. Now Squadron Leader RM Pugh AFC RAF Retd, he still enjoys retirement in Farnborough and unveiled the former Malvern Spitfire Team's memorial to his brother, Jack, in 1988.

Another Typhoon pilot was Pilot Officer John Thould, from Upton-upon-Severn in Worcestershire. He flew with 263 Squadron.

Whilst an NCO, Thould (back row, extreme left) attended No 25 Course at No 1 Special Low-level Attack Instructor's School. The signatures of his fellow students on the reverse appear to be JC Earle (3 Sqn), DH Sutherland (247), E Benn (186), S Bendle (181), KG Joachim (184) & EEG Noakes (245).

When Sergeant Thould reported for flying duties with 263 Squadron at Harrowbeer on February 27th, 1943, the unit was equipped with the Westland Whirlwind. A problematic aircraft known disrespectfully as the 'Crikey'.

Whirlwind photographs, especially from operational squadrons, are rare, so it is frustrating that John Thould did not caption these pictures in his album. Here an unknown pilot poses on a Whirlwind of 263 Squadron.

Another unknown 263 Squadron pilot. Again, note the rubber sleeves over each 20 mm cannon barrel.

Unknown 263 Squadron pilots before a sortie (note that the aircraft is bombed up).

John Thould (unusually wearing no rank insignia) helps arm his Whirlwind.

Typhoons replaced 263 Squadron's Whirlwinds in December 1943. Here the Squadron's pilots are pictured with a 'Bombphoon', John Thould at extreme left on wing.

Sergeants Thould, Handley and Cooper. The size of the Typhoon is apparent in this photograph.

Unknown 263 Squadron pilot in pre-invasion marking Typhoon.

Unknown 263 Squadron pilot, 1944.

Morale appears to have been high in 263!

Again, unknown 263 Squadron pilot.

263 Squadron Typhoon, 1944.

A clipped wing Spitfire Mk V, sporting unusual D-Day stripes. Details of the unit, circumstances and incident are unknown, but the photograph originates from John Thould's album.

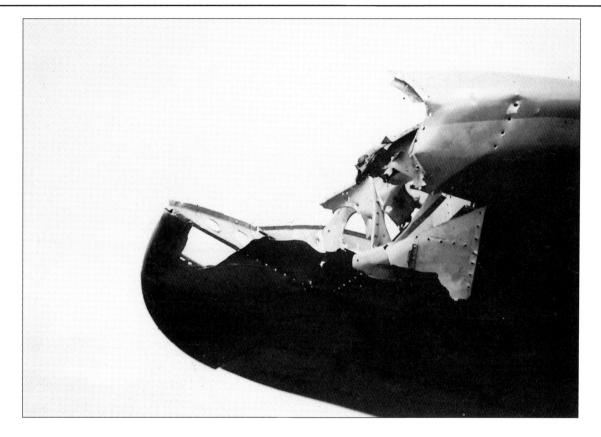

Pilot Officer Thould's MN476 after its wing tip was 'removed by a bofors shell' during a Ramrod, July 3rd, 1944.

MN476, The Hawk, prior to the application of D-Day stripes. Thould flew this Typhoon into action many times.

Sadly, Thould and The Hawk were fatally linked. On October 12th, 1944, Pilot Officer Thould flew as No 2 to the CO, Squadron Leader Rutter, during an attack on German artillery on the Belgian/German border. Hit by flak during the dive, MN476 crashed and the pilot was killed. John Thould was buried at Merksplas cemetery in Belgium, this being the original wooden marker.

Sergeant VJT 'Jack' Allen came from the tiny village of Hope-under-Dinmore, near Leominster in Herefordshire. He trained overseas, this photograph having been taken at No 1 OTU, Bagotville, Quebec, Canada.

Back in the UK, Sergeant Allen joined 616 Squadron at Culmhead, the unit operating the high-flying Spitfire Mk VII. During the build up to D-Day the Squadron was kept very busy, flying numerous Ramrods and hitting the enemy wherever he could be found. The 19-year old Sergeant Allen flew on many of these sorties.

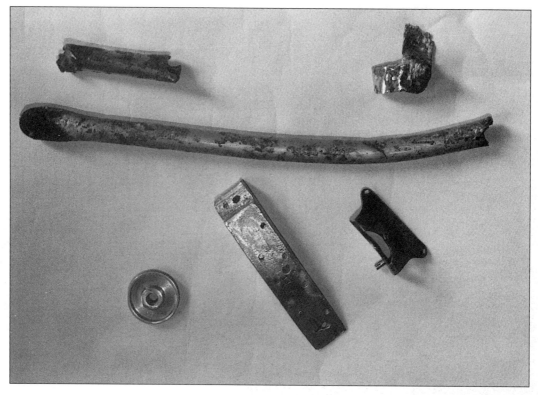

On June 29th, 1944, Sergeant Allen took off on a 'gunnery and aileron test flight to be carried out in the vicinity of the airfield'. He flew some distance north, however, and performed a low-level 'beat up' of his parents' Buskwood Farm. Tragically his family watched as Spitfire MB762 crashed on Dinmore Hill, the young pilot being killed outright. These items are all that now remains.

In 1988, the family having long since moved away, we found Sergeant Allen's grave in an overgrown state at St Mary's church, Hope-under-Dinmore. This we rectified. Sergeant Allen paid for his 'black' with his life, and the accident was used as an example to other headstrong pilots in the RAF training publication 'Tee-Emm'.

Moving on, little seems to be known about this French Spitfire pilot of 19 Squadron, Pilot Officer Rene Roger, pictured here in 1942, by the Squadron 'Spy', Flying Officer Winston Dilks.

Pilot Officer Tony Minchin was a VR pilot who joined 122 Squadron in March 1944. Flying the awesome Mustang, by the time his tour ended, Tony was strafing Luftwaffe air bases in Germany itself. He recalls being 'left standing' by an Me 262 jet that took off from Osnabrück.

Peter Taylor flew Spitfires and Mustangs with both 65 and 19 Squadron. He is pictured here in 1944 with a 65 Squadron Mustang.

The Mustang was probably the most offensive fighter of the Second World War. This example, of 19 Squadron, is fitted with auxiliary fuel tanks to extend range even further.

A section of 19 Squadron Mustang Mk IIIs on a sortie during 1944.

Flight Lieutenant THD Drinkwater DFC airborne in his 19 Squaron Mustang. 'Wilf' was his wife's nickname.

Drinkwater was a most experienced airman who joined the RAF as an Aircrafthand during the 1930s. By 1944, he was a Squadron Leader and CO of 122 Squadron with a DFC to his credit. Whilst flying Spitfires with 19 Squadron on January 7th, 1944, he was responsible for the destruction of the unit's 100th 'Hun'.

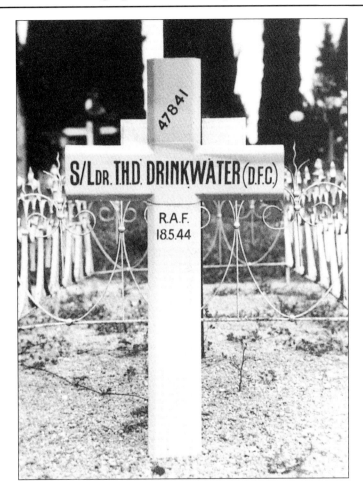

On May 18th, 1944, Squadron Leader Drinkwater's Mustang was brought down by flak and crashed near Nantes. 'Drink' was killed and buried in Sty Symhorien cemetery. In 1997, his brother, Les (who by coincidence served with my grandfather in the 3rd Grenadier Guards during 1940!) visited the area and unveiled a memorial to his elder brother which had been built by French enthusiasts. This was literally just in time, as Les died suddenly in August 1999.

Returning to Bob Beardsley's album, the next 14 photographs well illustrate the operating conditions of the pre and post D-Day period. After the Battle of Britain and sweeps of 1941, Bob served first as an instructor before returning to operations and involvement in the North African campaign. He next joined 222 Squadron, flying Spitfire Mk IXs, in time for the liberation of Europe. This photograph shows the pilots of 135 Wing, 84 Group, 2nd Tactical Air Force, comprising 33, 222 and 485 Squadrons.

Operating from the forward strip at Selsley Bill, shortly before D-Day: 'Self, Tony, Jack, Mac & Paddy'.

Even the Typhoon presence during this phase is illustrated in Bob's album: 'A Tiffy Rocketeer'.

'It's that flak again!'. A damaged 222 Squadron Spitfire Mk IX.

'My deputy upholding discipline!'

'The best bedroom! Mac, Woody & Junior'.

'Big Aussie Showoff!'

'Don't argue with the front end of a 190!'

'The pilots and other officers of 222 Squadron before leaving for Europe' (with OC Wing & W/Cdr Flying).

'The "Erks" of 222 , CO & OC Flights with 2 i/cs at Tangmere, Sussex'.

France at last: 'The only dry spot on Merville'.

'Dash & the secret weapon'.

'Wacko, Bill, Woody, Dash & Adjt.'

Although this book concentrates on RAF fighter pilots, former German Jagdflieger Hans 'Peter' Wulff became a great friend of mine. Peter flew He 111s in Russia before flying fighters in the west. Here he is pictured in his Me 410 of II/ZG26 in 1944.

Another shot of Peter in his 410. He is looking at the camera through his reflector gunsight, which in the 410 was roof mounted. An Me 410, painted in ZG26 colours, can be seen today at the Aerospace Museum, Cosford.

Leutnant Hans 'Peter' Wulff whilst flying FW190s with JG6. His wartime flying concluded on New Year's Day, 1945, when he was shot down by a Tempest over Holland and captured.

Sent to England as a prisoner, after the war Peter settled in Wales and married an English girl. He became a farmer and continued to fly for pleasure. Here he is pictured in 1995, at the launch of my fifth book, A Few of the Many, in which Peter's story was featured. This is how I will always remember Peter, smiling. Sadly he died in 1997, and it was a moving experience to speak at his funeral.

Less well documented than the European air war is that fought over the Far East by the 'Forgotten Air Force'. This is Squadron Leader TA 'Steve' Stevens, formerly a Spitfire pilot with 19 Squadron, leaving his P47 Thunderbolt. This is certainly an area of research well worth pursuing.

When the fighting was done. Squadron Leader Laurence Thorogood DFC and friends pose in a Spitfire graveyard in India, 1945. This is perhaps an appropriate note on which to end this particular Kaleidoscope, the first of a new series in which we will expand upon several of the themes herein.

Author's Postscript

The photographs in this book largely originate from the personal albums of survivors or casualties, and are therefore mostly personal snapshots taken with basic (now vintage) cameras. Although film was in short supply, and photography on service installations restricted, the number of private photographs taken never ceases to amaze. Books such as our Kaleidoscope series have facilitated the publication of many photographs that would not have otherwise been shared with the public. Many authors prefer using the high quality press images available to all via the Imperial War Museum or RAF Museum, but this has never appealed to me. Although the technical photographic quality of personal snaps are often lacking, especially when 60 years old, they still provide an accuracy and immediacy often so badly lacking in posed press shots.

When I first started seriously researching into the air war 1939-45, a main objective was to locate and copy as many of these photographs as possible, thus ensuring that whatever happened when their owner's passed away, they would not be lost to future generations. With that in mind, I would urge any veteran or relative who has any such photographs to contact me via Ramrod Publications. Originals are always treated with the utmost care and safely returned with the minimum of delay after copying. Naturally Ramrod Publications covers all costs.

The sad passing of Ron Rayner on April 8th, 1999, and numerous other WW2 fighter pilots and veteran friends since, has emphasised the importance of our work. All help with our race against time is therefore much appreciated and acknowledged.

Having written the foregoing towards the end of the Year 2000, on January 30th, 2001, I feel compelled to add that today, that great fighter pilot and friend Air Vice-Marshal JE 'Johnnie' Johnson has also passed away. The world, and in particular the aviation historical community, is now a much poorer place with this latest departure of a man who was possessed of true greatness. Rest in Peace, old friends, you deserve to.

The sadly late and much missed, Ron 'Cloudy' Rayner proudly poses with his DFC for my book A Few of the Many, in which he was featured. Until we met in 1992, however, Ron had told his story to no one. There must be many more veterans like him out there, modest men all seeking no recognition for themselves but all of whom with stories that must be recorded.